DEDICATION

To all those who strive for fulfillment in their careers,

This book is dedicated to you.

May its pages offer guidance, inspiration, and support

as you navigate the twists and turns of your professional journey.

Your dedication to finding meaning and satisfaction in your work

inspires us all to reach for our highest aspirations.

May you find fulfillment, purpose, and joy

in every step you take towards your dreams.

This is for you.

Find Fulfillment in Your Career

A Guide to Professional and Personal Success

Riley Anderson

Copyright © 2024 Riley Anderson

All rights reserved.

CONTENTS

ACKNOWLEDGMENTS 8

CHAPTER 1 10
Introduction: Why Fulfillment Matters 10
    1.1 What is Career Fulfillment? 10
    1.2 Why is Finding Fulfillment Important? 11
    1.3 The Impact of an Unfulfilling Career 12
    1.4 This Book's Roadmap to Fulfillment 13

CHAPTER 2 15
Self-Discovery: Uncovering Your Passions and Values 15
    2.1 Identifying Your Strengths and Skills 15
    2.2 Exploring Your Interests and Values 16
    2.3 Unmasking Your Limiting Beliefs 18
    2.4 Crafting a Personal Mission Statement 19

CHAPTER 3 21
Career Exploration: Unveiling the Landscape of Opportunities ... 21
    3.1 Researching Different Career Paths 21
    3.2 Informational Interviews: Learning from Others 22
    3.3 Skills Gap Analysis: Identifying What You Need 23
    3.4 Industry Trends: Aligning with the Future 24

CHAPTER 4 26
Goal Setting: Charting Your Course to Fulfillment 26
    4.1 Setting SMART Career Goals 26
    4.2 Breaking Down Long-Term Goals into Actionable Steps 27
    4.3 Prioritizing Goals and Overcoming Obstacles 29
    4.4 Creating a Personal Development Plan 30

CHAPTER 5 32
Building Your Network: Cultivating Connections 32
    5.1 The Power of Networking for Career Advancement 32
    5.2 Building Relationships with Mentors and Sponsors 33
    5.3 Leveraging Online Networking Platforms (e.g. LinkedIn) ... 35
    5.4 Effective Communication and Networking Etiquette 36

CHAPTER 6 38
The Job Search: Landing the Right Opportunity 38
6.1 Crafting a Compelling Resume and Cover Letter 38
6.2 Mastering the Art of Interviewing 40
6.3 Negotiating Your Salary and Benefits Package 41
6.4 Evaluating Job Offers: Finding the Best Fit 42

CHAPTER 7 44
Continuous Learning: Staying Ahead of the Curve 44
7.1 The Importance of Lifelong Learning in Today's Workplace 44
7.2 Identifying Learning Opportunities: Courses, Workshops, Conferences 46
7.3 Developing New Skills and Staying Current with Industry Trends 47
7.4 Building a Culture of Learning in Your Career 48

CHAPTER 8 50
Work-Life Balance: Achieving Harmony 50
8.1 Setting Boundaries and Managing Time Effectively 50
8.2 Prioritizing Your Well-being: Physical and Mental Health 51
8.3 Maintaining a Healthy Work-Life Balance for Long-Term Success 52
8.4 Combating Burnout and Maintaining Motivation 54

CHAPTER 9 56
Advocating for Yourself: Asking for What You Deserve 56
9.1 Negotiating Promotions and Raises with Confidence 56
9.2 Communicating Your Value and Achievements to Your Employer 57
9.3 Building Self-Confidence and Assertiveness in the Workplace 59
9.4 Setting Boundaries and Saying No When Necessary 60

CHAPTER 10 62
The Journey Continues: Maintaining Fulfillment Throughout Your Career 62
10.1 Adapting to Change and Embracing New Opportunities ... 62
10.2 Mentoring Others and Giving Back to Your Profession 63
10.3 Recognizing and Celebrating Your Achievements 64
10.4 Maintaining a Growth Mindset for Long-Term Fulfillment ... 66

Find Fulfillment in Your Career

ACKNOWLEDGMENTS

I would like to express my heartfelt gratitude to everyone who contributed to the creation of this book.

First and foremost, I am deeply thankful to my family for their unwavering support, patience, and encouragement throughout this journey. Your belief in me has been a constant source of strength.

I extend my sincere appreciation to my friends and colleagues who provided valuable insights, feedback, and encouragement along the way. Your perspectives enriched this project in ways I could never have imagined.

I am grateful to the mentors and educators who have guided and inspired me with their wisdom and expertise. Your mentorship has been instrumental in shaping my understanding of career fulfillment.

A special thank you to the readers who have embraced this book. Your curiosity and eagerness to learn motivate me to continue sharing knowledge and insights.

Lastly, I want to acknowledge the countless individuals who have shared their stories, experiences, and expertise in the field of career development. Your collective wisdom has laid the foundation for this work, and I am deeply grateful for your contributions.

Thank you all for being part of this journey.

CHAPTER 1

Introduction: Why Fulfillment Matters

Have you ever stared at the clock on a Monday morning, dreading the long week ahead? Or felt a constant sense of exhaustion despite getting enough sleep? If so, you're not alone. Millions of people around the world struggle with unfulfilling careers, a feeling that their work lacks meaning and purpose. But what exactly is career fulfillment, and why is it so important?

1.1 What is Career Fulfillment?

Career fulfillment is more than just a paycheck and a fancy title. It's about feeling a sense of satisfaction and purpose in your work. It's about using your skills and talents in a way that makes a positive impact and aligns with your values. It's about experiencing a sense of flow, where you're completely absorbed in a task and lose track of time because you're so engaged.

Here are some key aspects of career fulfillment:

1. Passion: You feel excited and motivated by your work.
2. Meaning: Your work contributes to something larger than yourself.
3. Growth: You have opportunities to learn and develop new skills.
4. Contribution: You feel valued and appreciated for your work.
5. Work-Life Balance: You can manage your work responsibilities without neglecting your personal life.

1.2 Why is Finding Fulfillment Important?

Finding fulfillment in your career has a ripple effect on your entire life. When you're passionate and engaged in your work, you:

- Experience greater well-being: Studies show a strong link between career fulfillment and increased happiness, reduced stress, and improved mental and physical health.
- Boost your productivity: When you're motivated and

engaged, you're naturally more productive and efficient at work.

- Enhance your creativity: A fulfilling career allows you to tap into your full potential and explore innovative ideas.
- Build stronger relationships: Feeling good about your work can positively impact your relationships with colleagues, friends, and family.
- Live a more meaningful life: Work takes up a significant portion of our lives. When your career is fulfilling, it contributes to a greater sense of purpose and overall satisfaction.

1.3 The Impact of an Unfulfilling Career

On the other hand, an unfulfilling career can have a significant negative impact on your life. You might experience:

- Chronic boredom and dissatisfaction: Feeling unchallenged and unmotivated can lead to a sense of apathy and stagnation.
- Burnout: Constant stress and pressure can lead to

emotional and physical exhaustion.

- Decreased productivity: If you're not engaged in your work, it's difficult to put in your best effort.
- Negative impact on health: Stress and dissatisfaction can lead to a variety of health problems, including anxiety, depression, and sleep disturbances.
- Strained relationships: Feeling frustrated with your work can negatively affect your interactions with colleagues and loved ones.

1.4 This Book's Roadmap to Fulfillment

You deserve a career that ignites your passion and fuels your purpose. This book is your roadmap to finding fulfillment in your work. We'll delve into the essential elements of career satisfaction, explore self-discovery tools, and provide practical strategies to navigate your career journey.

Throughout this journey, you'll learn how to:

1. Identify your strengths, values, and interests.
2. Explore different career paths and opportunities.
3. Set SMART career goals and develop a development

plan.
4. Craft a compelling resume and ace the job interview.
5. Maintain a healthy work-life balance and advocate for yourself.
6. Embrace continuous learning and adapt to change.

Following the steps outlined in this book, you'll be well on your way to building a fulfilling career that you can be truly proud of. Remember, your career is a journey, not a destination. This book will equip you with the tools and knowledge you need to navigate the road with confidence and find the path to lasting fulfillment.

CHAPTER 2

Self-Discovery: Uncovering Your Passions and Values

The foundation of a fulfilling career lies in self-discovery. Before you can chart a course towards your dream job, you need to understand who you are, what you value, and what lights you up. This chapter will guide you through a series of exercises to uncover your strengths, passions, and values, ultimately leading you to craft a personal mission statement that embodies your aspirations.

2.1 Identifying Your Strengths and Skills

Everyone has a unique set of strengths and skills. These are the things you're naturally good at and enjoy doing. Identifying your strengths is crucial because it allows you to leverage your capabilities and find a career path where you can excel.

Here are some ways to identify your strengths:

- Reflect on past experiences: Consider projects or activities where you felt energized, accomplished, and in the flow state. What skills did you use in those situations?
- Take a strengths assessment: Several online assessments can help you identify your dominant strengths based on personality traits or work styles.
- Seek feedback from others: Ask colleagues, mentors, and friends what they consider your strengths. You might be surprised by their insights.

Once you've identified your strengths, analyze how they translate into skills relevant to the workplace. For example, a strong analytical strength might translate into research skills, data analysis skills, or problem-solving skills.

2.2 Exploring Your Interests and Values

Your interests are the activities and subjects that naturally draw your curiosity and enthusiasm. When you explore your interests, you get a glimpse into what you find stimulating and engaging. Here are some ways to unearth your interests:

- Think about your hobbies and leisure activities: What do you do for fun in your free time? What topics do you find yourself frequently reading about or discussing?
- Consider past experiences: What projects or tasks have you enjoyed the most in your academic or professional career? What aspects of those experiences were most interesting to you?
- Imagine your ideal work environment: What kind of work environment would energize you? What type of problems would you like to solve? What kind of impact would you like to make?

Your values are the core principles that guide your decisions and actions. They represent what is most important to you in life. Understanding your values is crucial because you want your career to align with what you fundamentally believe in.

Here are some ways to explore your values:

- Brainstorm a list of important concepts: Consider

things like creativity, security, recognition, helping others, making a difference, etc.
- Prioritize your values: Rank the values on your list from most important to least important.
- Reflect on situations where you compromise your values: Think about times when you made a decision that went against your core beliefs. How did it make you feel?

2.3 Unmasking Your Limiting Beliefs

Limiting beliefs are negative thoughts and assumptions that hold you back from achieving your full potential. These beliefs can be formed by past experiences, societal expectations, or self-doubt. It's important to identify and challenge these beliefs so they don't hinder your career exploration. Here are some tips:

- Pay attention to your self-talk: What negative thoughts pop into your head when you think about your career?
- Challenge the evidence: Is there any evidence that supports your limiting beliefs? Are you basing them on facts or on fear?

- Reframe your thoughts: Replace negative beliefs with positive affirmations that empower you to move forward.

2.4 Crafting a Personal Mission Statement

A personal mission statement is a concise declaration that summarizes your core values, passions, and goals. It acts as a guiding light for your career decisions, helping you stay focused and motivated. Here are some steps to craft your own personal mission statement:

- Review your self-discovery exercises: Consider the strengths, interests, values, and goals you identified earlier.
- Draft a statement: Write a sentence or two that encapsulates what you want to achieve with your career and the impact you want to make.
- Refine and revise: Be clear, concise, and positive in your statement. Don't be afraid to revise it as your understanding of yourself and your goals evolves.

Your personal mission statement is a powerful tool for

self-discovery and career navigation. It will serve as a compass as you explore different career paths and opportunities.

By delving deep into yourself and uncovering your strengths, interests, and values, you'll gain a clear understanding of what truly makes you tick. This self-awareness is the foundation for building a fulfilling and meaningful career. Remember, the journey of self-discovery is ongoing. As you gain new experiences and learn more about yourself, your mission statement and career aspirations may evolve. Embrace this continuous exploration and use it to fuel your journey towards a fulfilling career.

CHAPTER 3

Career Exploration: Unveiling the Landscape of Opportunities

Armed with a newfound understanding of yourself, you're now ready to embark on the exciting journey of career exploration. The working world offers a vast landscape of possibilities, and this chapter will equip you with the tools to navigate it effectively.

3.1 Researching Different Career Paths

The first step is to broaden your horizons and explore the diverse range of career paths available. Here are some ways to delve into the world of work:

- Online resources: Utilize government websites focused on occupational information, career planning websites, and professional association websites to learn about different careers, their required skills, salary ranges, and job outlook. Career fairs and industry events:

Attend career fairs and industry events to network with professionals and gather information about specific job roles.

- Books and articles: Read books and articles about different careers or industries that pique your interest.
- Informational interviews: Conduct informational interviews with professionals in various fields to gain firsthand insights into their day-to-day work and career paths.

Don't limit yourself to traditional career paths. Consider the gig economy, freelancing opportunities, or starting your own business if these options align with your values and goals.

3.2 Informational Interviews: Learning from Others

Informational interviews are conversations with professionals in fields that interest you. These conversations are a fantastic way to learn about the realities of a particular job, gain valuable career advice, and potentially expand your network.

Here are some tips for conducting successful informational interviews:

- Identify potential interviewees: Look for professionals working in your target career path through LinkedIn, professional organizations, or alumni networks.
- Prepare insightful questions: Craft questions that demonstrate your genuine interest in the field and the professional's experience.
- Be respectful of their time: Keep your interview concise and focused. Express your gratitude for their time and insights.

Informational interviews are not job interviews. Your goal is to learn and gather information, not to apply for a specific position.

3.3 Skills Gap Analysis: Identifying What You Need

Through your self-discovery and research, you've identified potential career paths that align with your interests and values. Now, it's time to assess the skills required for those careers and compare them to your existing skill set.

Here's how to perform a skills gap analysis:

- List the essential skills for your target career: Identify the skills and experience most employers seek in job postings for your desired role.
- Inventory your own skills and experience: Make a list of your strengths, skills, and relevant experience you've gained through work, education, or volunteer activities.
- Identify the gaps: Compare your skills to the desired skills for your target career path. Where are the gaps?

Once you've identified the skills you need to develop, you can create a plan to bridge the gap. This might involve taking online courses, attending workshops, pursuing additional certifications, or volunteering to gain relevant experience.

3.4 Industry Trends: Aligning with the Future

The world of work is constantly evolving, and staying informed about industry trends is crucial for making informed career decisions.

Here are some ways to stay ahead of the curve:

- Follow industry publications and reports: Subscribe to newsletters or RSS feeds from industry publications and research firms to stay updated on the latest trends and developments.
- Attend industry conferences and webinars: Participating in conferences and webinars can provide valuable insights into industry trends and future skills needed.
- Network with professionals in your target field Connect with people working in your desired industry on LinkedIn or through professional organizations. They can offer valuable insights into the current state and future direction of their field.

By staying informed about industry trends, you can ensure that your skills and knowledge are aligned with the evolving needs of the workplace.

Career exploration is an ongoing process. Don't be afraid to explore different options and refine your goals as you learn more about yourself and the world of work. This chapter has equipped you with the tools to launch your exploration. In the next chapter, we'll delve into the art of setting SMART career goals and crafting a plan to achieve them.

CHAPTER 4

Goal Setting: Charting Your Course to Fulfillment

Now that you've embarked on your career exploration journey, it's time to translate your newfound knowledge and aspirations into concrete action. This chapter will guide you through the powerful process of setting SMART career goals and crafting a personalized development plan to achieve them.

4.1 Setting SMART Career Goals

Effective goal setting is the cornerstone of a successful career journey. SMART goals provide a clear roadmap, keeping you motivated and focused on achieving your desired outcomes. Here's how to set SMART career goals:

- Specific: Clearly define your goal. Instead of a vague desire to "advance in your career," state a specific objective like "obtain a promotion to senior software engineer within the next two years."

- **Measurable:** Establish clear criteria to track your progress. For your software engineer goal, measurable outcomes could be completing relevant training courses, acquiring a specific certification, or exceeding performance targets.
- **Attainable:** Set goals that are challenging yet achievable based on your current skills, resources, and time constraints. Stretch yourself, but don't set yourself up for failure.
- **Relevant:** Ensure your goals align with your overall career aspirations and values. Does a promotion to senior engineer truly align with your long-term career vision and sense of fulfillment?
- **Time-bound:** Set a realistic timeframe for achieving your goal. This creates a sense of urgency and helps you develop an action plan to reach your target date.

By following the SMART framework, you can ensure your career goals are well-defined, actionable, and aligned with your ultimate vision of success.

4.2 Breaking Down Long-Term Goals into Actionable Steps

Once you've established your SMART career goals, the next step is to break them down into smaller, more manageable tasks. This creates a clear action plan that guides your day-to-day activities and keeps you moving forward. Here's how to break down your goals:

- Identify key milestones: Divide your long-term goal into smaller, achievable milestones spaced throughout your timeframe.
- List required actions: For each milestone, identify the specific actions you need to take to achieve it. For example, to attain your senior engineer promotion within two years, actions might include enrolling in a coding bootcamp, shadowing senior engineers, and exceeding your quarterly performance goals.
- Prioritize your tasks: Not all actions will be created equal. Prioritize them based on their urgency and importance to achieving your overall goal.
- Set deadlines for each step: Assign realistic deadlines to each action to maintain accountability and momentum.

By breaking down your goals into actionable steps, you'll transform a seemingly overwhelming objective into a series of achievable tasks that will keep you motivated and on track.

4.3 Prioritizing Goals and Overcoming Obstacles

With a multitude of goals and tasks, it's natural to feel overwhelmed. Prioritization is crucial for managing your time and energy effectively.

- Identify your core goals: Analyze your list and identify the 2-3 most critical goals that will have the most significant impact on your career journey.
- Schedule time for your top priorities: Block time in your calendar specifically dedicated to working on your core goals and prioritized tasks.
- Learn to say no: Don't be afraid to politely decline requests or commitments that don't align with your top priorities.
- Anticipate obstacles: Challenges and setbacks are inevitable. Identify potential roadblocks you might encounter and brainstorm strategies to overcome them in advance.

Remember, flexibility is key. As you progress, adapt your plan if necessary, but always stay focused on your core goals and remain persistent in the face of obstacles.

4.4 Creating a Personal Development Plan

Now that you have SMART career goals and a plan of action, it's time to create a personalized development plan (PDP) to guide your journey. Your PDP is a living document that outlines your skills development strategy aligned with your career goals. Here's what to include:

- Your career goals: Briefly restate your SMART career goals at the top of your PDP.
- Learning activities: List the specific learning activities you'll undertake to bridge your skill gaps, such as online courses, workshops, professional certifications, or mentorship opportunities.
- Resources: Identify resources needed to support your learning activities, including tuition costs for courses, books, software licenses, or conference fees.
- Timeline: Integrate the timelines for your action steps

and learning activities into your PDP to ensure you're on track.

- Progress tracking: Establish a system for tracking your progress towards your goals and learning objectives.

CHAPTER 5

BUILDING YOUR NETWORK: CULTIVATING CONNECTIONS

In today's competitive job market, your skills and experience are only part of the equation. A strong professional network can be a game-changer, opening doors to new opportunities, providing valuable career advice, and even influencing hiring decisions. This chapter will guide you on building a robust network of professional connections to fuel your career journey.

5.1 The Power of Networking for Career Advancement

Networking is more than just collecting business cards. It's about cultivating genuine relationships with people in your field. These connections can offer a wealth of benefits:

- Job opportunities: Your network can be a valuable source of job leads and referrals. People in your network may be aware of upcoming openings or recommend you for positions within their companies.

- Industry insights: Network connections can provide you with valuable insights into industry trends, career paths, and company cultures.
- Mentorship and guidance: Experienced professionals in your network can offer invaluable mentorship, providing career advice, feedback, and support.
- Increased confidence: Building relationships with others in your field can boost your confidence and self-belief as you navigate your career path.

Investing time and effort in building your network is an investment in your future success.

5.2 Building Relationships with Mentors and Sponsors

Mentors and sponsors are two distinct yet crucial players in your network.

Mentors: Mentors are experienced professionals who offer guidance and support on your career path. They can provide advice on skill development, navigating workplace dynamics, and achieving your long-term goals.

Sponsors: Sponsors are influential figures who actively

advocate for you and your career advancement. They might recommend you for promotions, connect you with key decision-makers, or endorse your skills and experience to others.

Identifying Mentors and Sponsors:

Look for mentors and sponsors within your professional network – colleagues, former supervisors, professors, or industry leaders. Consider their expertise, career trajectory, and personality when seeking mentorship.

Building Strong Relationships:

- Be proactive: Take the initiative to reach out to potential mentors and sponsors.
- Do your research: Learn about their background and areas of expertise.
- Offer value: Demonstrate that you're a valuable addition to their network. What can you learn from them, and what can you offer in return?
- Communicate effectively: Maintain regular communication with your mentors and sponsors.

Update them on your progress and express your gratitude.

Building strong mentoring and sponsorship relationships takes time and effort. Be patient, respectful, and provide value in return for their guidance and support.

5.3 Leveraging Online Networking Platforms (e.g. LinkedIn)

Online platforms like LinkedIn are powerful tools for building and expanding your professional network. Here's how to leverage them effectively:

- Craft a compelling profile: Create a professional profile that showcases your skills, experience, and accomplishments.
- Join relevant groups: Engage with online groups related to your field. Participate in discussions, share your expertise, and connect with other professionals.
- Follow industry influencers: Follow thought leaders and companies you admire to stay updated on industry trends and connect with relevant individuals.
- Connect with former colleagues and classmates:

Reconnect with past colleagues and classmates on LinkedIn. These connections can be a valuable source of support and potential leads.

Utilize online platforms strategically to connect with a wider audience and expand your network reach.

5.4 Effective Communication and Networking Etiquette

Building your network is not just about connecting; it's about effective communication and proper etiquette. Here are some key points to remember:

- Be clear and concise: When reaching out to someone, clearly state your purpose for connecting and what you hope to gain from the interaction.
- Be respectful of others' time: Keep your initial communication brief and offer to schedule a more detailed conversation if appropriate.
- Maintain a professional demeanor: Be mindful of your online presence and communication style.
- Follow up graciously: After connecting with someone, send a thank-you note or email expressing your

appreciation for their time and insights.

Following these principles, you'll create positive and lasting impressions that will strengthen your network and open doors to new opportunities.**

Building a strong network takes time and consistent effort, but the rewards are substantial. As you cultivate genuine relationships, you'll gain valuable support, access to knowledge and opportunities, and ultimately accelerate your journey towards career fulfillment. The next chapter will delve into the art of crafting a compelling resume and acing the job interview, equipping you with the skills to navigate your career path with confidence.

CHAPTER 6

The Job Search: Landing the Right Opportunity

Now that you've embarked on a journey of self-discovery, explored career options, and built a strong network, it's time to translate your aspirations into action. This chapter equips you with the tools to navigate the job search effectively, from crafting compelling application materials to landing the perfect opportunity that aligns with your goals and values.

6.1 Crafting a Compelling Resume and Cover Letter

Your resume and cover letter are your first impression to potential employers. Here's how to craft documents that showcase your skills and experience and secure that coveted interview:

Resume:

Tailor your resume for each job application. Highlight the skills and experiences most relevant to the specific position and company.

Focus on achievements, not just responsibilities. Quantify your accomplishments whenever possible. Use action verbs and metrics to demonstrate the impact you made in previous roles.

Maintain a clear and concise format. Use a professional and easy-to-read layout. Proofread meticulously for any typos or grammatical errors.

Cover Letter:

Personalize each cover letter. Address the letter to a specific hiring manager whenever possible. Research the company and tailor your message to their needs and culture.

Highlight your unique value proposition. Explain why you're the ideal candidate for the role. Connect your skills and experience to the specific requirements and challenges mentioned in the job description.

Keep it concise and engaging. Aim for a one-page cover letter that is clear, concise, and free of clichés.

By investing time and effort into crafting strong application materials, you'll increase your chances of standing out from the competition and landing that coveted interview.

6.2 Mastering the Art of Interviewing

The job interview is your opportunity to shine and showcase your skills and personality. Here are some tips to ensure a successful interview:

- Preparation is key: Research the company, the position, and the interviewer beforehand. Prepare insightful questions to demonstrate your genuine interest in the opportunity.
- Dress professionally: First impressions matter. Dress appropriately for the company culture while maintaining a professional appearance.
- Arrive early and be confident: Punctuality and confidence go a long way. Project a positive and enthusiastic demeanor throughout the interview.
- Actively listen and respond thoughtfully: Pay close attention to the interviewer's questions and respond clearly and concisely. Highlight relevant skills and experiences that demonstrate your qualifications.
- Ask insightful questions: Prepare questions that

showcase your interest in the role, the company culture, and the opportunity for growth.
- Follow up with a thank-you note: Express your gratitude for the interviewer's time and reiterate your interest in the position.

Remember, the interview is a two-way street. While you're being evaluated, you're also evaluating the company and the role to determine if it's a good fit for you.

6.3 Negotiating Your Salary and Benefits Package

Once you receive a job offer, congratulations! But before you accept, take the time to carefully consider the compensation and benefits package. Here's how to approach salary negotiations effectively:

- Do your research: Research average salary ranges for the specific position and location. Consider factors like your experience level, industry standards, and the company's size and profitability.
- Understand the entire offer: The compensation package goes beyond just the base salary. Consider

health insurance plans, retirement contributions, paid time off, and other benefits offered.

- Be confident and professional: Clearly articulate your desired salary range and justification based on your skills and experience. Be prepared to negotiate, but do so respectfully and professionally.
- Don't be afraid to walk away: If the offer doesn't meet your expectations or align with your needs, don't be afraid to politely decline and continue your job search.

By understanding your worth and negotiating effectively, you can secure a compensation package that reflects your value and contributes to your overall career satisfaction.

6.4 Evaluating Job Offers: Finding the Best Fit

Receiving multiple job offers is a fantastic outcome. However, choosing the right opportunity requires careful consideration. Here are some factors to evaluate:

- Alignment with your career goals: Does the position align with your long-term career aspirations and values?

- Company culture: Research the company culture and ensure it's a positive environment where you can thrive.
- Growth opportunities: Does the role offer opportunities for learning, development, and advancement?
- Compensation and benefits: Compare the total compensation packages offered by each company, including salary, benefits, and work-life balance considerations.

Ultimately, the best job offer is the one that best aligns with your overall career goals, values, and well-being. Don't be afraid to ask follow-up questions to clarify any aspects of the job offers or company culture. Trust your gut instinct and choose the opportunity that excites you the most and feels like the right fit for the next chapter in your career journey.

CHAPTER 7

CONTINUOUS LEARNING: STAYING AHEAD OF THE CURVE

The world of work is constantly evolving. New technologies emerge, industries adapt, and skills requirements shift. This makes lifelong learning an essential aspect of career success in today's dynamic environment. This chapter will explore the significance of continuous learning, identify valuable learning opportunities, and guide you on building a growth mindset for your career journey.

7.1 The Importance of Lifelong Learning in Today's Workplace

Gone are the days when you could learn a skill set upon entering the workforce and expect it to serve you throughout your entire career. Here's why continuous learning is crucial for professional success:

- Maintaining Your Competitive Edge: New skills and

knowledge are constantly in demand. Continuous learning allows you to stay relevant in your field and competitive in the job market.

- Adapting to Change: The pace of change in today's workplace is rapid. Lifelong learning equips you with the agility to adapt to new technologies, processes, and industry trends.
- Enhancing Your Skills and Expertise: By continuously learning, you expand your skills and deepen your expertise, making you a more valuable asset to your current or future employers.
- Boosting Creativity and Innovation: Learning new things stimulates your mind, fosters creativity, and allows you to approach challenges and opportunities with fresh perspectives.
- Increasing Your Earning Potential: Employees with in-demand skills and knowledge often command higher salaries and have greater career advancement opportunities.

Investing in continuous learning is an investment in your long-term career success and overall professional fulfillment.

7.2 Identifying Learning Opportunities: Courses, Workshops, Conferences

Fortunately, there are numerous avenues for lifelong learning available:

- Formal Education: Consider pursuing additional degrees, certifications, or online courses to deepen your knowledge and acquire new skills.
- Professional Development Programs: Many companies offer training programs and workshops for their employees. Take advantage of these opportunities to develop relevant skills.
- Industry Conferences and Events: Attending industry conferences and events allows you to stay current with trends, network with professionals, and learn from experts in your field.
- Online Resources: A wealth of online resources like tutorials, webinars, and ebooks can provide valuable learning opportunities on a variety of topics.
- Mentorship and Coaching: Seek guidance from mentors or coaches who can share their knowledge and expertise and help you navigate your career path.

The key is to be proactive in identifying and pursuing learning opportunities that align with your career goals and skill development needs.

7.3 Developing New Skills and Staying Current with Industry Trends

Once you've identified valuable learning opportunities, it's time to translate them into action. Here are some tips for effective learning:

- Set SMART learning goals: Just like career goals, establish clear and achievable learning objectives for yourself. What specific skills do you want to develop? By when?
- Create a learning plan: Develop a plan that outlines the learning resources you'll utilize, the time commitment required, and the milestones you'll aim to achieve.
- Be an active learner: Don't just passively consume information. Engage actively with the learning materials, participate in discussions, and practice your

newly acquired skills.

- Seek out challenges: Step outside your comfort zone and challenge yourself to learn new things. This will accelerate your growth and development.
- Stay updated on industry trends: Continuously monitor industry publications, attend conferences, and network with professionals to stay informed about the latest trends and developments.

By actively engaging in the learning process, you'll ensure that your skills and knowledge remain current and relevant in the ever-evolving landscape of your chosen field.

7.4 Building a Culture of Learning in Your Career

Lifelong learning shouldn't be a one-time event; it should be an ongoing habit.

Here's how to foster a culture of learning in your career:

- Develop a growth mindset: Embrace the belief that your skills and knowledge can be continuously developed through effort and learning.

- Allocate dedicated learning time: Schedule time in your calendar specifically for learning activities, whether it's reading industry publications, taking online courses, or attending workshops.
- Seek out learning opportunities in your daily work: Look for opportunities to learn from colleagues, volunteer for new projects, or take on challenging tasks.
- Celebrate your learning achievements: Acknowledge and reward yourself for your learning accomplishments. This will keep you motivated to continue expanding your knowledge and skills.

By integrating continuous learning into your professional life, you'll cultivate a growth mindset that fosters ongoing development, innovation, and ultimately, career success.

CHAPTER 8

WORK-LIFE BALANCE: ACHIEVING HARMONY

The pursuit of a fulfilling career doesn't have to come at the expense of your personal well-being. This chapter explores the concept of work-life balance, providing strategies to achieve harmony between your professional and personal life for long-term success and overall satisfaction.

8.1 Setting Boundaries and Managing Time Effectively

Creating a healthy work-life balance often starts with establishing clear boundaries. Here's how to achieve this:

- Communicate your boundaries: Clearly communicate your work hours and availability to colleagues, managers, and clients. Respect your designated off-work time as much as you respect your work commitments.
- Learn to say no: Don't be afraid to politely decline additional work or commitments that would

overwhelm your schedule and personal life.

- Prioritize ruthlessly: Not all tasks are created equal. Learn to prioritize tasks based on urgency and importance and delegate or eliminate non-essential activities.
- Manage your time effectively: Utilize time management techniques to maximize your productivity during work hours. This allows you to leave work on time and disconnect to focus on your personal life.

By setting boundaries and managing your time effectively, you can regain control over your schedule and ensure you have dedicated time for both work and personal pursuits.

8.2 Prioritizing Your Well-being: Physical and Mental Health

Your well-being is the foundation for a successful and fulfilling career. Here's why prioritizing your health is crucial:

- Improved Physical Health: Maintaining a healthy lifestyle through regular exercise, balanced nutrition, and adequate sleep improves your energy levels, reduces stress, and enhances overall well-being.

- **Enhanced Mental Health:** Prioritizing activities that manage stress, promote relaxation, and nurture your mental well-being is essential for focus, creativity, and resilience in the workplace.
- **Increased Productivity and Creativity:** Taking care of yourself physically and mentally leads to improved focus, enhanced problem-solving skills, and increased creative thinking.
- **Reduced Risk of Burnout:** Prioritizing your well-being helps prevent burnout, a state of emotional exhaustion and cynicism that can significantly impact your work performance and overall health.

Investing in your well-being is not a luxury; it's a necessity for long-term career success and overall life satisfaction.

8.3 Maintaining a Healthy Work-Life Balance for Long-Term Success

Achieving work-life balance is an ongoing process, not a one-time destination. Here are some tips for maintaining a healthy balance:

- Schedule personal time: Just like you schedule work meetings, schedule dedicated time for personal activities, hobbies, and spending time with loved ones.
- Disconnect from work: Set boundaries around technology use. Avoid checking work emails or taking work calls outside of designated work hours. Disconnecting allows you to be fully present in your personal life.
- Maintain a flexible mindset: Be prepared to adapt your schedule as needed. Unexpected events arise, so be flexible and adjust your approach to maintain a healthy balance.
- Communicate with your employer: Open communication with your employer can lead to flexible work arrangements or adjustments that can contribute to a healthier work-life balance.

A healthy work-life balance is not about achieving a perfect 50/50 split. It's about finding a balance that works for you and allows you to thrive in both your professional and personal spheres.

8.4 Combating Burnout and Maintaining Motivation

Even with the best intentions, burnout can creep in. Here's how to recognize it and maintain motivation:

- Recognize the signs of burnout: These include emotional exhaustion, cynicism towards work, reduced sense of accomplishment, and physical or emotional problems.
- Take proactive steps: If you experience burnout symptoms, address them immediately. Take time off, delegate tasks, and prioritize your well-being.
- Find sources of motivation: Reconnect with your career goals and passions. Seek inspiration from mentors, colleagues, or industry leaders.
- Celebrate your achievements: Acknowledge and celebrate your accomplishments, big or small. This reinforces a sense of purpose and keeps you motivated.

By recognizing the signs of burnout and proactively taking steps to maintain your motivation, you can ensure long-term career satisfaction and continued engagement in your professional journey.

CHAPTER 9

ADVOCATING FOR YOURSELF: ASKING FOR WHAT YOU DESERVE

Throughout your career journey, you'll encounter situations where advocating for yourself is essential. This chapter empowers you with the tools and strategies to confidently negotiate promotions, raises, and effectively communicate your value to your employer.

9.1 Negotiating Promotions and Raises with Confidence

Negotiating promotions and raises can feel daunting, but with preparation and confidence, you can achieve successful outcomes. Here's how to approach these conversations effectively:

- Do your research: Research average salary ranges for your position, experience level, and location. Gather data on industry benchmarks and your company's performance to strengthen your case.
- Document your achievements: Maintain a record of

your accomplishments, exceeding targets, and contributions to the company's success. Use specific metrics and data to quantify your impact.

- Practice your pitch: Rehearse your negotiation points beforehand. Clearly articulate the value you bring to the company and why you deserve a promotion or raise.
- Be confident and professional: Project confidence in your abilities and the value you offer. Maintain a professional demeanor throughout the negotiation process.
- Be prepared to walk away: Know your bottom line and be prepared to walk away if the offer doesn't meet your expectations.

By advocating for yourself with confidence and a well-prepared case, you increase your chances of securing a promotion or a raise that reflects your worth.

9.2 Communicating Your Value and Achievements to Your Employer

Effective communication is key to ensuring your employer

recognizes your contributions and value. Here are some tips:

- Schedule regular performance reviews: Don't wait for your annual review to discuss your accomplishments. Proactively schedule meetings with your manager to highlight your achievements and contributions.
- Quantify your impact: Use data and metrics to showcase the positive outcomes of your work. Demonstrate how your efforts have benefited the company.
- Tailor your communication: Adapt your communication style to your manager's preferences. Some may prefer concise emails, while others might appreciate detailed reports.
- Seek feedback and ask for opportunities: Express your desire for growth and development. Ask for feedback on your performance and inquire about opportunities to take on new challenges or responsibilities.

By consistently communicating your value and seeking growth opportunities, you position yourself for advancement and recognition within the company.

9.3 Building Self-Confidence and Assertiveness in the Workplace

Advocating for yourself requires self-confidence and assertiveness. Here's how to cultivate these qualities:

- Identify your strengths and accomplishments: Reflect on your skills, knowledge, and past achievements. Acknowledge your strengths and the value you bring to the table.
- Challenge negative self-talk: Replace negative self-beliefs with positive affirmations. Focus on your capabilities and potential.
- Practice assertive communication: Develop clear and concise communication skills. Express your needs, opinions, and requests directly and respectfully.
- Role-play negotiation scenarios: Practice how you'll handle difficult conversations with colleagues or managers. Role-playing builds confidence and hones your negotiation skills.
- Seek out mentors and role models: Find mentors or role models who demonstrate assertiveness and strong communication skills. Learn from their experience and

approach.

By actively building your self-confidence and assertiveness, you'll be better equipped to advocate for yourself effectively in the workplace.

9.4 Setting Boundaries and Saying No When Necessary

Setting boundaries and saying no are essential aspects of advocating for yourself. Here's how to approach them:

- Be clear about your limitations: Recognize your capacity and workload. Don't be afraid to decline additional tasks or projects if it would overload you.
- Offer alternative solutions: When declining a request, consider offering alternative solutions or suggest delegating tasks to maintain a healthy workload.
- Use assertive language: When saying no, be clear, concise, and professional. Explain your reasoning and avoid making excuses.
- Focus on the positive: Frame your refusal in a positive light. For example, "I appreciate the opportunity, but I currently have my hands full with X project. Perhaps

we can revisit this in the future?"

Setting boundaries and saying no allows you to prioritize your well-being and manage your workload effectively. This, in turn, fosters better performance and reduces the risk of burnout.

Advocating for yourself is not about being pushy or demanding. It's about confidently communicating your value, setting healthy boundaries, and ensuring you're recognized and rewarded for your contributions. By mastering these skills, you'll empower yourself to navigate your career path with greater confidence and achieve your desired outcomes.

CHAPTER 10

THE JOURNEY CONTINUES: MAINTAINING FULFILLMENT THROUGHOUT YOUR CAREER

Congratulations! You've embarked on a journey of self-discovery, explored career options, navigated the job search, and equipped yourself with the tools for success. But remember, your career is a lifelong adventure, filled with continuous learning, growth, and opportunities to make a positive impact. This chapter explores strategies to maintain a sense of fulfillment and keep your career journey exciting and rewarding over the long term.

10.1 Adapting to Change and Embracing New Opportunities

The world of work is constantly evolving. New technologies emerge, industries shift, and job requirements transform. Here's how to embrace change and thrive in a dynamic professional landscape:

- Maintain a growth mindset: Believe that your skills

and knowledge can be continuously developed. Embrace challenges as opportunities to learn and grow.
- Stay informed about industry trends: Continuously monitor industry publications abreast of the latest developments.
- Be open to new opportunities: Don't be afraid to step outside your comfort zone and explore new possibilities. New challenges and roles can lead to unexpected discoveries and career growth.
- Develop your adaptability skills: Learn to be flexible and adjust your approach as needed. Embrace change as a natural part of the professional journey.

By cultivating a growth mindset and remaining adaptable, you'll be well-positioned to navigate change and seize new opportunities that keep your career path stimulating and fulfilling.

10.2 Mentoring Others and Giving Back to Your Profession

As you gain experience and expertise, consider mentoring others. Here's how sharing your knowledge can benefit both you and your profession:

- Empowering the next generation: Mentoring future professionals allows you to share your knowledge, offer guidance, and help shape the next generation of your field.
- Gaining new perspectives: Mentoring can be a two-way street. You might learn new approaches or gain fresh perspectives from your mentees.
- Strengthening your network: Mentoring relationships expand your professional network and connect you with like-minded individuals.
- Building a sense of purpose: Giving back to your profession through mentorship fosters a sense of purpose and contributes to the overall growth of your field.

Mentoring is a valuable way to share your expertise, contribute to your profession, and gain personal satisfaction from helping others succeed.

10.3 Recognizing and Celebrating Your Achievements

Taking the time to acknowledge your accomplishments is crucial for maintaining motivation and a sense of fulfillment. Here's how to celebrate your wins:

- Reflect on your progress: Regularly take time to reflect on your career journey. Acknowledge how far you've come and the skills you've developed.
- Celebrate both big and small wins: Don't wait for major milestones. Take the time to celebrate both large achievements and the completion of smaller projects or tasks.
- Reward yourself: Acknowledge your accomplishments with meaningful rewards. This reinforces a sense of satisfaction and motivates you to keep striving.
- Share your successes with loved ones: Let your supportive network know about your achievements. Sharing your success strengthens relationships and fosters a sense of accomplishment.

Recognizing and celebrating your wins, you'll maintain a positive attitude, boost your confidence, and stay motivated throughout your career journey.

10.4 Maintaining a Growth Mindset for Long-Term Fulfillment

A growth mindset is essential for achieving long-term career fulfillment. Here's how to cultivate and maintain it:

- Embrace challenges: View challenges as opportunities to learn and develop new skills. Don't shy away from difficulties; see them as stepping stones to growth.
- Focus on learning, not just outcomes: Success is not just about achieving the end goal; it's about the journey and the knowledge gained along the way.
- Celebrate effort and perseverance: Acknowledge your hard work and dedication as much as the final results. Perseverance and continuous effort are key to long-term success.
- Seek continuous learning: Never stop learning and expanding your knowledge base. Remain curious and actively seek opportunities for personal and professional development.

Embracing a growth mindset, you'll cultivate a lifelong love of learning, maintain a sense of purpose, and ensure your career journey remains an exciting and rewarding adventure.

ABOUT THE AUTHOR

Riley Anderson is a multifaceted individual, blending the roles of business guru, writer, and motivational speaker. With a keen insight into the intricacies of publishing and a talent for inspiring others, Riley has become a sought-after figure in both the literary and entrepreneurial worlds.

In terms of education, Riley holds a degree in Business Administration with a focus on Marketing from a reputable university. This educational background, coupled with years of practical experience, has equipped Riley with the knowledge and skills needed to navigate the competitive landscape of both the business and publishing industries. Whether through written works or captivating speeches,

Riley's aim is to empower and guide individuals on their journey to success

www.ingramcontent.com/pod-product-compliance
Lightning Source LLC
Chambersburg PA
CBHW050239230526
45470CB00005B/2026